EASY CHICKEN THIGH COOKBOOK

50 UNIQUE AND EASY CHICKEN THIGH RECIPES

2nd Edition

By
BookSumo Press
Copyright © by Saxonberg Associates

Published by
BookSumo Press, a DBA of Saxonberg Associates
http://www.booksumo.com/

ABOUT THE AUTHOR.

BookSumo Press is a publisher of unique, easy, and healthy cookbooks.

Our cookbooks span all topics and all subjects. If you want a deep dive into the possibilities of cooking with any type of ingredient. Then BookSumo Press is your go to place for robust yet simple and delicious cookbooks and recipes. Whether you are looking for great tasting pressure cooker recipes or authentic ethic and cultural food. BookSumo Press has a delicious and easy cookbook for you.

With simple ingredients, and even simpler step-by-step instructions BookSumo cookbooks get everyone in the kitchen chefing delicious meals.

BookSumo is an independent publisher of books operating in the beautiful Garden State (NJ) and our team of chefs and kitchen experts are here to teach, eat, and be merry!

INTRODUCTION

Welcome to *The Effortless Chef Series*! Thank you for taking the time to purchase this cookbook.

Come take a journey into the delights of easy cooking. The point of this cookbook and all BookSumo Press cookbooks is to exemplify the effortless nature of cooking simply.

In this book we focus on cooking with Chicken Thighs. You will find that even though the recipes are simple, the taste of the dishes are quite amazing.

So will you take an adventure in simple cooking? If the answer is yes please consult the table of contents to find the dishes you are most interested in.

Once you are ready, jump right in and start cooking.

— BookSumo Press

TABLE OF CONTENTS

Any Issues? Contact Us

If you find that something important to you is missing from this book please contact us at info@booksumo.com.

We will take your concerns into consideration when the 2nd edition of this book is published. And we will keep you updated!

— BookSumo Press

LEGAL NOTES

COMMON ABBREVIATIONS

cup(s)	C.
tablespoon	tbsp
teaspoon	tsp
ounce	oz.
pound	lb

*All units used are standard American measurements

CHAPTER 1: EASY CHICKEN THIGH RECIPES

MANDARIN CHICKEN

Ingredients

- 1 C. orange juice
- 1 tbsp soy sauce
- 1 (1 oz.) envelope dry onion soup mix
- 1/2 tsp garlic powder, or to taste
- 8 chicken thighs

Directions

- Set your oven to 350 degrees before doing anything else.
- Get a bowl, combine: garlic powder, orange juice, onion soup, and soy sauce.
- Clean your chicken under fresh cold water then enter them into a casserole dish.
- Top the chicken pieces with the onion soup mix.
- Now cook everything in the oven for 90 mins.
- Baste the chicken every 20 mins. Enjoy.

Amount per serving (8 total)

Timing Information:

Preparation	5 m
Cooking	1 h 30 m
Total Time	1 h 35 m

Nutritional Information:

Calories	180 kcal
Fat	9.9 g
Carbohydrates	5.7g
Protein	16.4 g
Cholesterol	59 mg
Sodium	475 mg

* Percent Daily Values are based on a 2,000 calorie diet.

HONEY AND SRIRACHA CHICKEN

Ingredients

- 1/2 C. rice vinegar
- 5 tbsps honey
- 1/3 C. soy sauce (such as Silver Swan(R))
- 1/4 C. Asian (toasted) sesame oil
- 3 tbsps Sriracha
- 3 tbsps minced garlic
- salt to taste
- 8 skinless, boneless chicken thighs
- 1 tbsp chopped green onion (optional)

Directions

- Get a bowl, combine: salt, vinegar, garlic, honey, sriracha, soy sauce, and sesame oil.
- Divide the sauce amongst two bowls.
- Put your chicken pieces into one of the bowls, then evenly coat them with sauce, and place them in the fridge, with a covering of plastic, for 60 mins.
- Set your oven to 425 degrees before doing anything else.

- Now a get a pan and boil the remaining half of the marinade for 4 mins while stirring.
- Now put your chicken in a casserole dish and top with one third of the sauce in the pan.
- Cook everything in the oven for 35 mins and baste every 10 mins.
- Let the chicken sit for 15 mins while you get your sauce heated again. Once it is hot again top the chicken with the rest of the hot sauce.
- Enjoy.

Amount per serving (4 total)

Timing Information:

Preparation	5 m
Cooking	30 m
Total Time	1 h 40 m

Nutritional Information:

Calories	544 kcal
Fat	30.2 g
Carbohydrates	26.6g
Protein	40.6 g
Cholesterol	142 mg
Sodium	1814 mg

* Percent Daily Values are based on a 2,000 calorie diet.

SYRUP SRIRACHA CHICKEN

Ingredients

- 1 clove garlic, sliced, or more to taste
- 2 tsps Asian chili pepper sauce, sriracha
- 1 1/2 tbsps maple syrup
- 2 tbsps soy sauce
- 2 tbsps mayonnaise
- 3 tbsps rice vinegar
- salt and freshly ground black pepper to taste
- 2 lbs skinless, boneless chicken thighs
- 1 lime, cut into 8 wedges

Directions

- Place your garlic in a bowl and mash it until pasty.
- Then add in: vinegar, chili pepper sauce, mayo, syrup, and soy sauce.
- Place your chicken thighs in a casserole dish and top them with the garlic sauce.
- Place some plastic around the dish and chill everything it in the fridge for 3 hours.
- Then add some salt to it.

- Grill your chicken pieces for 4 mins per side.
- Then continue cooking for about 8 more mins flipping the chicken every 2 or 3 mins.
- Garnish your chicken with lime wedges.
- Enjoy.

Amount per serving (8 total)

Timing Information:

Preparation	15 m
Cooking	20 m
Total Time	3 h 40 m

Nutritional Information:

Calories	194 kcal
Fat	10.8 g
Carbohydrates	4g
Protein	19.5 g
Cholesterol	71 mg
Sodium	311 mg

* Percent Daily Values are based on a 2,000 calorie diet.

CREAMY MUSHROOMS AND ONIONS

Ingredients

- 8 chicken thighs
- 1 tbsp vegetable oil
- 1 pinch ground black pepper
- 1 pinch salt
- 1 pinch paprika
- 1 (10.75 oz.) can condensed cream of mushroom soup
- 1 (1 oz.) package dry onion soup mix
- 1 C. sour cream
- 1 tbsp lemon juice
- 1 tsp dried dill weed

Directions

- Get a frying and pan and with some hot oil brown the chicken all over.
- Then add everything to a casserole dish and top with paprika, pepper, and salt.
- Get a bowl, combine: dill, mushroom soup, lemon juice, onion soup, and sour cream.

- Combine everything until smooth and evenly top your chicken with this mix.
- Cook the contents in the oven for 60 mins.
- Enjoy.

Amount per serving (4 total)

Timing Information:

Preparation	10 m
Cooking	1 h
Total Time	1 h 20 m

Nutritional Information:

Calories	637 kcal
Fat	48.8 g
Carbohydrates	12.7g
Protein	36.1 g
Cholesterol	183 mg
Sodium	1284 mg

* Percent Daily Values are based on a 2,000 calorie diet.

FRENCH STYLE CHICKEN AND APRICOTS

Ingredients

- 12 chicken thighs
- 1 C. apricot preserves
- 1 C. French dressing
- 1 (1 oz.) package dry onion soup mix

Directions

- Set your oven to 350 degrees before doing anything else.
- Get a bowl, combine: soup, apricots, and dressing.
- Get a casserole dish and place your chicken in it then top with the apricot mix.
- Cook everything in the oven for 1 h.
- Enjoy.

Amount per serving (12 total)

Timing Information:

Preparation	10 m
Cooking	1 h
Total Time	1 h 20 m

Nutritional Information:

Calories	342 kcal
Fat	20.1 g
Carbohydrates	23.3g
Protein	15.9 g
Cholesterol	59 mg
Sodium	444 mg

* Percent Daily Values are based on a 2,000 calorie diet.

Dijon, Brown Sugar, and Cayenne Chicken

Ingredients

- 8 large bone-in, skin-on chicken thighs
- 1/2 C. Dijon mustard
- 1/4 C. packed brown sugar
- 1/4 C. red wine vinegar
- 1 tsp dry mustard powder
- 1 tsp salt
- 1 tsp freshly ground black pepper
- 1/2 tsp ground dried chipotle pepper
- 1 pinch cayenne pepper, or to taste
- 4 cloves garlic, minced
- 1 onion, sliced into rings
- 2 tsps vegetable oil, or as needed

Directions

- Get a bowl, combine: cayenne, Dijon, chipotle, vinegar, black pepper, mustard powder, and salt.
- Take your chicken and cut some incisions in them (at least 2). Then place everything in the bowl.
- Place a covering of plastic around the bowl, and put everything in the fridge for 5 to 8 hrs.

- Cover a casserole dish with foil and then set your oven to 450 degrees before doing anything else.
- Pour your onions around the dish and then layer the chicken on top.
- Coat everything with some veggies and top the contents with some cayenne and salt.
- Cook everything in the oven for 50 mins.
- Then plate the chicken.
- Now boil the drippings for 5 mins while stirring.
- Finally top the chicken and onions with the sauce.
- Enjoy.

Amount per serving (8 total)

Timing Information:

Preparation	20 m
Cooking	40 m
Total Time	5 h

Nutritional Information:

Calories	352 kcal
Fat	19 g
Carbohydrates	13.8g
Protein	29.1 g
Cholesterol	106 mg
Sodium	765 mg

* Percent Daily Values are based on a 2,000 calorie diet.

Onions, Carrots, and Rosemary Chicken

Ingredients

- 6 chicken thighs
- salt and ground black pepper to taste
- 1 yellow onion, diced
- 1/4 C. chopped fresh basil, or to taste
- 3 cloves garlic, sliced
- 2 tsps finely chopped fresh rosemary
- 1 1/2 C. chicken broth
- 3 C. diced carrots

Directions

- Set your oven to 375 degrees before doing anything else.
- Place your chicken in a casserole dish and then top everything with: rosemary, basil, garlic, carrots, pepper, salt, and onions.
- Now cover everything in the broth.
- Wrap some foil around the top of the casserole dish and cook the contents in the oven for 65 mins.
- After 65 mins has elapsed remove the covering on the dish and continue cooking for 10 more mins. Enjoy.

Amount per serving (6 total)

Timing Information:

Preparation	15 m
Cooking	1 h 10 m
Total Time	1 h 25 m

Nutritional Information:

Calories	238 kcal
Fat	12.2 g
Carbohydrates	10.8g
Protein	20.6 g
Cholesterol	72 mg
Sodium	352 mg

* Percent Daily Values are based on a 2,000 calorie diet.

AMERICAN STYLE BAKE CHICKEN I

Ingredients

- cooking spray
- 8 bone-in chicken thighs with skin
- 1/4 tsp garlic salt
- 1/4 tsp onion salt
- 1/4 tsp dried oregano
- 1/4 tsp ground thyme
- 1/4 tsp paprika
- 1/4 tsp ground black pepper

Directions

- Get a casserole dish and then line it with foil and nonstick spray.
- Now set your oven to 350 degrees before doing anything else.
- Get a bowl, mix: pepper, garlic salt, paprika, onion salt, thyme, and oregano.
- Place your chicken in the dish and top with the spice mix.
- Cook everything in the oven for 65 mins.
- Enjoy.

Amount per serving (8 total)

Timing Information:

Preparation	10 m
Cooking	1 h
Total Time	1 h 10 m

Nutritional Information:

Calories	190 kcal
Fat	11.9 g
Carbohydrates	0.2g
Protein	19.2 g
Cholesterol	71 mg
Sodium	178 mg

* Percent Daily Values are based on a 2,000 calorie diet.

Indian Style Chicken I
(Tandoori)

Ingredients

- 2 (6 oz.) containers plain yogurt
- 2 tsps kosher salt
- 1 tsp black pepper
- 1/2 tsp ground cloves
- 2 tbsps freshly grated ginger
- 3 cloves garlic, minced
- 4 tsps paprika
- 2 tsps ground cumin
- 2 tsps ground cinnamon
- 2 tsps ground coriander
- 16 chicken thighs
- olive oil spray

Directions

- Get a bowl, combine: garlic, ginger, paprika, yogurt, cumin, cloves, cinnamon, salt, coriander, and pepper.
- Clean your chicken pieces and then place them in the bowl with the yogurt.
- Coat the chicken evenly and place a covering on the bowl.
- Put everything in the fridge overnight.

- Grill your chicken pieces after topping them with some oil for 3 mins over direct heat, then flip and grill for 3 more mins.
- Place the chicken to the side of the grill over non direct heat and let it cook for 45 mins.
- Enjoy with cooked basmati rice.

Amount per serving (8 total)

Timing Information:

Preparation	10 m
Cooking	45 m
Total Time	8 h 55 m

Nutritional Information:

Calories	349 kcal
Fat	20.5 g
Carbohydrates	5.4g
Protein	34.2 g
Cholesterol	120 mg
Sodium	618 mg

* Percent Daily Values are based on a 2,000 calorie diet.

JAPANESE STYLE CHICKEN I

Ingredients

- 1 tbsp cornstarch
- 1 tbsp cold water
- 1/2 C. white sugar
- 1/2 C. soy sauce
- 1/4 C. cider vinegar
- 1 clove garlic, minced
- 1/2 tsp ground ginger
- 1/4 tsp ground black pepper
- 12 skinless chicken thighs

Directions

- Get the following boiling with a medium to low level of heat: black pepper, cornstarch, ginger, water, vinegar, sugar, and soy sauce.
- Once the sauce is thick and has reduced a bit set your oven to 425 degrees before doing anything else.
- Enter your chicken into a casserole dish and top liberally with the thick sauce, then flip each piece and top with more sauce.
- Cook everything in the oven for 35 mins.
- Baste the chicken with the sauce every 7 mins.
- Enjoy.

Amount per serving (6 total)

Timing Information:

Preparation	30 m
Cooking	1 h
Total Time	1 h 30 m

Nutritional Information:

Calories	272 kcal
Fat	9.8 g
Carbohydrates	19.9g
Protein	24.7 g
Cholesterol	85 mg
Sodium	1282 mg

* Percent Daily Values are based on a 2,000 calorie diet.

HONEY MUSTARD AND CURRY CHICKEN

Ingredients

- 1 (3 lb) whole chicken, cut into pieces
- 1/2 C. butter, melted
- 1/2 C. honey
- 1/4 C. prepared mustard
- 1 tsp salt
- 1 tsp curry powder

Directions

- Set your oven to 350 degrees before doing anything else.
- Get a bowl, mix: curry, melted butter, salt, honey, and mustard.
- Enter your chicken into a casserole dish and then top everything with all the honey sauce.
- Cook the chicken in the oven for 80 mins.
- While the chicken is cooking baste it every 10 mins.
- Enjoy.

Amount per serving (6 total)

Timing Information:

Preparation	15 m
Cooking	1 h 15 m
Total Time	1 h 30 m

Nutritional Information:

Calories	514 kcal
Fat	32.9 g
Carbohydrates	24g
Protein	31.3 g
Cholesterol	138 mg
Sodium	709 mg

* Percent Daily Values are based on a 2,000 calorie diet.

Soy Sauce and Parsley Chicken

Ingredients

- 1/2 C. butter
- 3 tbsps minced garlic
- 3 tbsps soy sauce
- 1/4 tsp black pepper
- 1 tbsp dried parsley
- 6 boneless chicken thighs, with skin
- dried parsley, to taste

Directions

- Get a casserole dish or broiler pan and coat it with oil or nonstick spray.
- Now turn on your ovens broiler to low if possible before doing anything else.
- Get a bowl, combine: parsley, butter, pepper, garlic, and soy sauce.
- Place it in the microwave for 3 mins.
- Place your chicken in the dish and top the chicken with the microwave mix.
- Leave some of the mix for basting during the cooking time.

- Cook the chicken under the broiler for 25 mins and turn the chicken half way through the cooking time.
- Now baste the chicken with the rest of the mix.
- Before serving add a garnishing of parsley.
- Enjoy.

Amount per serving (6 total)

Timing Information:

Preparation	10 m
Cooking	20 m
Total Time	30 m

Nutritional Information:

Calories	303 kcal
Fat	25.1 g
Carbohydrates	2.3g
Protein	16.8 g
Cholesterol	99 mg
Sodium	615 mg

* Percent Daily Values are based on a 2,000 calorie diet.

RED POTATOES AND PARSLEY CHICKEN

Ingredients

- 8 chicken thighs
- 6 small red potatoes, quartered
- 1/2 C. extra-virgin olive oil, or as needed
- 1 tbsp chopped fresh rosemary
- 1 1/2 tsps chopped fresh oregano
- 1 1/2 tsps garlic powder
- salt and pepper to taste

Directions

- Set your oven to 375 degrees before doing anything else.
- Get a bowl, add in: potatoes, chicken, and olive oil.
- Place everything into a casserole dish and top with: pepper, rosemary, salt, garlic powder, and oregano.
- Cook everything in the oven for 65 mins with a covering of foil around the dish and then 10 mins with no cover.
- Enjoy.

Amount per serving (6 total)

Timing Information:

Preparation	15 m
Cooking	1 h
Total Time	1 h 15 m

Nutritional Information:

Calories	497 kcal
Fat	31.9 g
Carbohydrates	27.6g
Protein	24.4 g
Cholesterol	78 mg
Sodium	81 mg

* Percent Daily Values are based on a 2,000 calorie diet.

INDIAN STYLE CHICKEN II (MAKHANI) (BUTTER CHICKEN)

Ingredients

- 1 tbsp peanut oil
- 1 shallot, finely chopped
- 1/4 white onion, chopped
- 2 tbsps butter
- 2 tsps lemon juice
- 1 tbsp ginger garlic paste
- 1 tsp garam masala
- 1 tsp chili powder
- 1 tsp ground cumin
- 1 bay leaf
- 1/4 C. plain yogurt
- 1 C. half-and-half
- 1 C. tomato puree
- 1/4 tsp cayenne pepper, or to taste
- 1 pinch salt
- 1 pinch black pepper
- 1 tbsp peanut oil
- 1 lb boneless, skinless chicken thighs, cut into bite-size pieces
- 1 tsp garam masala
- 1 pinch cayenne pepper
- 1 tbsp cornstarch
- 1/4 C. water

Directions

- Stir fry your onions and shallots in oil for 2 mins then add in: bay leaf, butter, cumin, lemon juice, chili powder, ginger-garlic paste, garam masala.
- Cook for 1 more min before adding: yoghurt and half and half.
- Get everything boiling and then gently simmer with a low level of heat for 12 mins while stirring.
- Now add in pepper and salt.
- Place the mix to the side and get a new pan.
- Add in 1 tbsp of oil and brown your chicken in the oil for 12 mins. Now lower the heat, and add in 1 tsp of masala and cayenne and a few tbsps of sauce.
- Let the chicken lightly boil in the sauce until fully done.
- Now add in the rest of the sauce.
- Finally combine in some water and cornstarch and cook everything for 12 mins until it all becomes thick.
- Enjoy.

Amount per serving (4 total)

Timing Information:

Preparation	10 m
Cooking	25 m
Total Time	35 m

Nutritional Information:

Calories	408 kcal
Fat	27.8 g
Carbohydrates	15.6g
Protein	23.4 g
Cholesterol	107 mg
Sodium	523 mg

* Percent Daily Values are based on a 2,000 calorie diet.

MEXICAN CHICKEN FAJITAS

Ingredients

- 1 tbsp Worcestershire sauce
- 1 tbsp cider vinegar
- 1 tbsp soy sauce
- 1 tsp chili powder
- 1 clove garlic, minced
- 1 dash hot pepper sauce
- 1 1/2 lbs boneless, skinless chicken thighs, cut into strips
- 1 tbsp vegetable oil
- 1 onion, thinly sliced
- 1 green bell pepper, sliced
- 1/2 lemon, juiced

Directions

- Get a bowl, combine: hot sauce, Worcestershire, chicken, garlic, vinegar, chili powder, and soy sauce.
- Make sure the chicken pieces are evenly covered then place some plastic around the bowl.
- Let the chicken sit in the sauce for 40 mins on the counter or in the fridge.
- Stir fry your chicken pieces for 7 mins then combine in the green peppers and onions. Cook for 4 more mins and garnish the meat with some lemon.
- Serve with warmed tortillas. Enjoy.

Amount per serving (5 total)

Timing Information:

Preparation	15 m
Cooking	10 m
Total Time	55 m

Nutritional Information:

Calories	210 kcal
Fat	8.3 g
Carbohydrates	5.7g
Protein	27.6 g
Cholesterol	113 mg
Sodium	344 mg

* Percent Daily Values are based on a 2,000 calorie diet.

FRIED AND BAKED CHICKEN

Ingredients

- 12 chicken thighs
- 3 eggs
- 1 C. all-purpose flour
- 1 C. Italian seasoned bread crumbs
- salt and pepper to taste
- 1 tsp paprika
- 1/2 C. vegetable oil

Directions

- Set your oven to 350 degrees before doing anything else.
- Get a bowl, add in: flour, pepper, and salt.
- Get a 2nd bowl, add: bread crumbs.
- Get a 3rd bowl for your whisked eggs.
- Dip the chicken in the flour, then into the eggs, and finally in the bread crumbs.
- Get a casserole dish and add in the oil and then the chicken and top with paprika.

- Cook everything in the oven for 35 mins then flip the chicken and continue cooking for 30 more mins.
- Place the chicken on paper towels for 10 mins before serving.
- Enjoy.

Amount per serving (10 total)

Timing Information:

Preparation	10 m
Cooking	1 h 30 m
Total Time	1 h 40 m

Nutritional Information:

Calories	310 kcal
Fat	15.1 g
Carbohydrates	18g
Protein	23.8 g
Cholesterol	126 mg
Sodium	296 mg

* Percent Daily Values are based on a 2,000 calorie diet.

JAPANESE STYLE CHICKEN II

Ingredients

- 1 C. soy sauce
- 1 C. brown sugar
- 1 C. water
- 4 cloves garlic, minced
- 1 onion, chopped
- 1 tbsp grated fresh ginger root
- 1 tbsp ground black pepper
- 1 tbsp dried oregano
- 1 tsp crushed red pepper flakes (optional)
- 1 tsp ground cayenne pepper (optional)
- 1 tsp ground paprika (optional)
- 5 lbs skinless chicken thighs

Directions

- Get a bowl, combine: paprika, soy sauce, cayenne, sugar, pepper flakes, water, oregano, garlic, black pepper, onions, and ginger.
- Now add the chicken and stir everything.
- Place a covering on the bowl, and place it in the fridge for 60 mins.
- Grill your chicken pieces for 16 mins each side.
- Enjoy.

Amount per serving (12 total)

Timing Information:

Preparation	
Cooking	30 m
Total Time	1 h 30 m

Nutritional Information:

Calories	338 kcal
Fat	12.6 g
Carbohydrates	21.7g
Protein	33.4 g
Cholesterol	114 mg
Sodium	1304 mg

* Percent Daily Values are based on a 2,000 calorie diet.

Spanish Chicken

Ingredients

- 1 tbsp olive oil
- 3 lbs skinless chicken thighs
- salt and ground black pepper to taste
- 1/4 C. loosely packed cilantro leaves
- 2 large sweet potatoes, cut into chunks
- 1 red bell pepper, cut into strips
- 2 (15.5 oz.) cans black beans, rinsed and drained
- 1/2 C. chicken broth
- 1/4 C. loosely packed cilantro leaves
- 1 C. hot salsa
- 2 tsps ground cumin
- 1/2 tsp ground allspice
- 3 large cloves garlic, chopped
- lime wedges, for garnish

Directions

- Top your chicken pieces with pepper, 1/4 cilantro, and salt before browning them in olive oil for 6 mins per side.
- Place the chicken pieces in the crock pot as well as: black beans, garlic, broth, allspice, 1/4 cilantro, cumin, salsa, potatoes, and bell peppers.
- Cook everything on low for 5 hrs then garnish with some lime.
- Enjoy.

Amount per serving (6 total)

Timing Information:

Preparation	25 m
Cooking	4 h 10 m
Total Time	4 h 35 m

Nutritional Information:

Calories	591 kcal
Fat	18.1 g
Carbohydrates	56.9g
Protein	50.2 g
Cholesterol	1137 mg
Sodium	980 mg

* Percent Daily Values are based on a 2,000 calorie diet.

Soy Sauce, Honey, and Basil Chicken

Ingredients

- 4 skinless, boneless chicken thighs
- 1/2 C. soy sauce
- 1/2 C. ketchup
- 1/3 C. honey
- 3 cloves garlic, minced
- 1 tsp dried basil

Directions

- Get a bowl, mix: basil, soy sauce, garlic, ketchup, and honey.
- Add your chicken to the slow cooker as well as the honey sauce and cook for 6 hours with a low level of heat.
- Enjoy.

Amount per serving (4 total)

Timing Information:

Preparation	10 m
Cooking	6 h
Total Time	6 h 10 m

Nutritional Information:

Calories	325 kcal
Fat	11.9 g
Carbohydrates	34.2g
Protein	21.9 g
Cholesterol	71 mg
Sodium	2204 mg

* Percent Daily Values are based on a 2,000 calorie diet.

EASY SESAME CHICKEN

Ingredients

- 4 C. vegetable oil for frying
- 1 egg
- 1 1/2 lbs boneless, skinless chicken thighs, cut into 1/2 inch cubes
- 1 tsp salt
- 1 tsp white sugar
- 1 pinch white pepper
- 1 C. cornstarch
- 2 tbsps vegetable oil
- 3 tbsps chopped green onion
- 1 clove garlic, minced
- 6 dried whole red chilies
- 1 strip orange zest
- 1/2 C. white sugar
- 1/4 tsp ground ginger
- 3 tbsps chicken broth
- 1 tbsp rice vinegar
- 1/4 C. soy sauce
- 2 tsps sesame oil
- 2 tbsps peanut oil
- 2 tsps cornstarch
- 1/4 C. water
- 2 tbsps sesame seeds

Directions

- Get your oil to 375 degrees in a big pan before doing anything else
- Get a bowl, combine: white pepper, whisked eggs, salt, and chicken.
- Add in the cornstarch 1 tsp at a time and stir constantly.

- Fry your chicken, in batches, until golden in the oil for about 4 mins each.
- Then place everything to the side.
- Once all the batches have been fried.
- Fry them again for 1 to 2 mins each.
- Then place the fried pieces on some paper towels.
- Get another pan and add in 2 tbsps of veggie oil and stir fry the following in it for 3 mins: orange zest, green onions, chilies, and garlic.
- Now add in: peanut oil, half a C. of sugar, sesame oil, ginger, soy sauce, broth, and vinegar.
- Get everything boiling and let it cook for 4 mins.
- Add in 2 tsps of cornstarch with some water and then add this to the sauce and get it boiling again for 2 more mins.
- Add the chicken in, set the heat to low, and let the sauce combine into the chicken.
- Let everything cook for about 2 more mins then top with sesame seeds.
- Enjoy.

Amount per serving (6 total)

Timing Information:

Preparation	25 m
Cooking	25 m
Total Time	50 m

Nutritional Information:

Calories	634 kcal
Fat	36.5 g
Carbohydrates	54.9g
Protein	24.3 g
Cholesterol	101 mg
Sodium	1192 mg

* Percent Daily Values are based on a 2,000 calorie diet.

Homemade BBQ Sauce Chicken

Ingredients

- 4 tbsps water
- 3 tbsps ketchup
- 3 tbsps brown sugar
- 2 tbsps vinegar
- 1 tbsp lemon juice
- 2 tbsps Worcestershire sauce
- 1 tsp salt
- 1 tsp dry mustard
- 1 tsp chili powder
- 12 chicken thighs, skin removed

Directions

- Set your oven to 500 degrees before doing anything else.
- Get the following boiling for 2 mins: chili powder, water, mustard powder, ketchup, salt, sugar, Worcestershire, vinegar, and lemon juice.
- Once everything is boiling reduce the heat and let it gently cook for 17 mins.
- Add your chicken to a casserole dish and top it with the sauce.
- Place a covering of foil around the dish and cook everything the oven for 17 mins.
- Now set the heat to 200 degrees and cook for 65 more mins.
- Take off the cover and finally let the chicken cook for 10 more mins to get crunchy. Enjoy.

Amount per serving (12 total)

Timing Information:

Preparation	20 m
Cooking	1 h 30 m
Total Time	1 h 50 m

Nutritional Information:

Calories	135 kcal
Fat	7.3 g
Carbohydrates	5.1g
Protein	11.8 g
Cholesterol	43 mg
Sodium	306 mg

* Percent Daily Values are based on a 2,000 calorie diet.

Hawaiian Style Chicken

Ingredients

- 1 tbsp vegetable oil
- 10 boneless, skinless chicken thighs
- 3/4 C. honey
- 3/4 C. lite soy sauce
- 3 tbsps ketchup
- 2 cloves garlic, crushed
- 1 tbsp minced fresh ginger root
- 1 (20 oz.) can pineapple tidbits, drained with juice reserved
- 2 tbsps cornstarch
- 1/4 C. water

Directions

- Get a bowl, combine: pineapple juice, honey, ginger, soy sauce, garlic, and ketchup.
- Brown your chicken for about 5 mins per side, in oil, then add them to your slow cooker. Now top everything with pineapple sauce.

- With a high level of heat let this cook for 4 hrs then take out the thighs, add in the pineapple and mix in the water and cornstarch. Let the sauce get thick.
- When serving your chicken top liberally with sauce.
- Enjoy.

Amount per serving (10 total)

Timing Information:

Preparation	20 m
Cooking	4 h
Total Time	4 h 20 m

Nutritional Information:

Calories	235 kcal
Fat	6 g
Carbohydrates	34.4g
Protein	13 g
Cholesterol	42 mg
Sodium	724 mg

* Percent Daily Values are based on a 2,000 calorie diet.

Indian Style Chicken III (Makhani) (Slow Cooker)

Ingredients

- 2 tbsps butter
- 2 tbsps vegetable oil
- 4 large skinless, boneless chicken thighs, cut into bite-sized pieces
- 1 onion, diced
- 3 cloves garlic, minced
- 2 tsps curry powder
- 1 tbsp curry paste
- 2 tsps tandoori masala
- 1 tsp garam masala
- 1 (6 oz.) can tomato paste
- 15 green cardamom pods
- 1 C. low-fat plain yogurt
- 1 (14 oz.) can coconut milk
- salt to taste

Directions

- Stir fry your garlic, onions, and chicken in veggie oil and butter for 12 mins then add in: tomato paste, curry powder and paste, garam masala, and tandoori masala.
- Cook and stir fry, the mix for 3 mins until smooth, then add everything into your slow cooker.

- Add in: yogurt, cardamom, and coconut milk as well as pepper and salt to the mix and cook everything for 8 hrs on low.
- Enjoy with basmati rice.

Amount per serving (6 total)

Timing Information:

Preparation	15 m
Cooking	4 h 15 m
Total Time	4 h 30 m

Nutritional Information:

Calories	480 kcal
Fat	33.3 g
Carbohydrates	17.2g
Protein	30.6 g
Cholesterol	103 mg
Sodium	442 mg

* Percent Daily Values are based on a 2,000 calorie diet.

ARABIC AND LATIN FUSION CHICKEN

Ingredients

- 2 tbsps vegetable oil
- 1 onion, grated
- 2 cloves garlic, chopped
- 1 1/2 lbs boneless skinless chicken thighs, cut in half
- 3 tsps ground turmeric
- 1 tsp chili powder
- 1 1/2 tsps salt
- 1 (14.5 oz.) can peeled and diced tomatoes
- 2 tbsps ghee (clarified butter)
- 3 tsps ground cumin
- 3 tsps ground coriander
- 2 tbsps grated fresh ginger root
- 1/2 C. chopped cilantro leaves

Directions

- Stir fry your garlic and onions for 4 mins in oil then combine in the salt, tomatoes, chicken, chili powder, and turmeric.
- Get everything boiling, place a lid on the pan, set the heat to low, and cook for 22 mins.
- Remove the lid and cook the contents for 12 more mins to let most of the liquid cook out.
- Combine in: cilantro, ghee, ginger, cumin, and coriander.

- Now cook the mix for 6 more mins before serving with a topping of sauce.
- Enjoy.

Amount per serving (6 total)

Timing Information:

Preparation	20 m
Cooking	55 m
Total Time	1 h 15 m

Nutritional Information:

Calories	265 kcal
Fat	16.9 g
Carbohydrates	6.7g
Protein	20.4 g
Cholesterol	79 mg
Sodium	755 mg

* Percent Daily Values are based on a 2,000 calorie diet.

BACON AND POTATOES CHICKEN

Ingredients

- 6 chicken thighs
- 6 chicken drumsticks
- 12 slices center-cut bacon
- salt and black pepper to taste
- 1 onion, coarsely chopped
- 1 1/2 lbs baby Dutch yellow potatoes

Spice Mix:

- 2 tbsps dried chives
- 2 tbsps dried basil
- 1 tbsp garlic powder
- 1 tbsp adobo seasoning
- 1 tbsp ground black pepper
- 1 tsp salt, or to taste

Directions

- Set your oven to 400 degrees before doing anything else.
- Get your chicken and cover it with a piece of bacon then layer your chicken pieces in a casserole dish after topping them with onions, pepper, and salt.
- Get a bowl, mix: black pepper, chives, adobo, basil, and garlic powder.
- Add the potatoes around the chicken in the casserole dish and top everything with the chive spice mix.
- Cook the chicken and potatoes in the oven for 65 mins then top with more salt. Enjoy.

Amount per serving (6 total)

Timing Information:

Preparation	20 m
Cooking	1 h
Total Time	1 h 20 m

Nutritional Information:

Calories	548 kcal
Fat	27.7 g
Carbohydrates	24.6g
Protein	48.2 g
Cholesterol	155 mg
Sodium	1012 mg

* Percent Daily Values are based on a 2,000 calorie diet.

Jalapenos, Peanuts, and Ginger Chicken

Ingredients

- 3/4 C. dark brown sugar
- 1/3 C. cold water
- 1/3 C. fish sauce
- 1/3 C. rice vinegar
- 1 tbsp soy sauce
- 4 cloves garlic, crushed
- 1 tbsp fresh grated ginger
- 1 tsp vegetable oil

- 8 boneless, skinless chicken thighs, quartered
- 1/2 C. roasted peanuts
- 2 fresh jalapeno peppers, seeded and sliced
- 1 bunch green onions, chopped
- fresh cilantro sprigs, for garnish

Directions

- Get a bowl, combine: ginger, brown sugar, garlic, water, soy sauce, vinegar, and fish sauce.
- Stir fry your chicken, in oil, for 3 mins, then add in 1/3 of a C. of the ginger mix, and cook for 8 mins until thick.
- Now add in the rest of the mix and cook for 7 more mins until the chicken is fully done.
- Once it is done add: onions, jalapenos, and peanuts.

- Heat everything for 4 mins then top everything with some cilantro.
- Enjoy.

Amount per serving (4 total)

Timing Information:

Preparation	20 m
Cooking	20 m
Total Time	40 m

Nutritional Information:

Calories	615 kcal
Fat	33.2 g
Carbohydrates	37.9g
Protein	43 g
Cholesterol	129 mg
Sodium	1967 mg

* Percent Daily Values are based on a 2,000 calorie diet.

BUTTERY MUSHROOM BAKE

Ingredients

- 8 chicken thighs
- 1 (10.75 oz.) can condensed cream of mushroom soup
- 10 oz. milk
- 1 tsp dried parsley
- 1/2 tsp onion powder
- 1 C. dry bread crumbs
- 2 tbsps melted butter
- 1 tsp cornstarch

Directions

- Set your oven to 350 degrees before doing anything else.
- Get a bowl, add in: soup, milk, onion powder, and parsley.
- Get a 2nd bowl for the bread crumbs.
- Coat the chicken with the milk mix and then some bread crumbs.
- Put everything into a casserole dish that has been coated with nonstick spray.
- Top the chicken with the butter and cook it all in the oven for 50 mins.

- Simultaneously combine the cornstarch and the rest of the soup in a small pan and stir until boiling. Once it is boiling, set the heat to low and cook for 3 mins until it becomes thick.
- Garnish your chicken with the hot soup mix.
- Enjoy.

Amount per serving (4 total)

Timing Information:

Preparation	15 m
Cooking	45 m
Total Time	1 h

Nutritional Information:

Calories	575 kcal
Fat	32.7 g
Carbohydrates	29g
Protein	39 g
Cholesterol	138 mg
Sodium	868 mg

* Percent Daily Values are based on a 2,000 calorie diet.

SUNBELT CLASSIC CHICKEN

Ingredients

- 3 lbs chicken thighs
- 2 tbsps soy sauce
- 1/2 C. ketchup
- 1/4 C. corn syrup
- 1 pinch garlic powder

Directions

- Set your oven to 350 degrees before doing anything else.
- Get a bowl, combine: garlic powder, soy sauce, corn syrup, and ketchup.
- Clean your chicken and then place all the pieces in a casserole dish.
- Now top everything with the soy mix.
- Cook the chicken in the oven for 65 mins.
- Baste the meat at least 3 times before it finishes cooking.
- Enjoy.

Amount per serving (4 total)

Timing Information:

Preparation	10 m
Cooking	1 h
Total Time	1 h 10 m

Nutritional Information:

Calories	807 kcal
Fat	52 g
Carbohydrates	23.1g
Protein	59.9 g
Cholesterol	1286 mg
Sodium	1044 mg

* Percent Daily Values are based on a 2,000 calorie diet.

CREAMY ONIONS

(SLOW COOKER)

Ingredients

- 8 skinless, boneless chicken thighs halves
- 4 potatoes, cubed
- 1 (10.75 oz.) can condensed cream of mushroom soup
- 1 1/3 C. milk
- 1 tbsp cornstarch
- 1 (1 oz.) package dry onion soup mix

Directions

- Get a bowl, mix: soup mix, mushroom soup, cornstarch, and milk.
- Add the potatoes to the crock pot as well as the chicken.
- Top the chicken with the soup mix.
- Place a lid on the slow cooker and let it cook for 9 hrs with a low level of heat.
- Enjoy.

Amount per serving (5 total)

Timing Information:

Preparation	10 m
Cooking	10 h
Total Time	10 h 10 m

Nutritional Information:

Calories	444 kcal
Fat	7.5 g
Carbohydrates	41.9g
Protein	50.5 g
Cholesterol	1115 mg
Sodium	1048 mg

* Percent Daily Values are based on a 2,000 calorie diet.

CHICKEN AND RICE

Ingredients

- 2 cubes chicken bouillon
- 1 tbsp water
- 1 C. uncooked white rice
- 1/4 C. butter
- 1 onion, chopped
- 2 C. water
- 6 chicken thighs
- 1 tsp Italian-style seasoning

Directions

- Set your oven to 350 degrees before doing anything else.
- Get a bowl, mix: 2 C. of water, onion, bouillon, butter, and rice.
- Layer the rice, once it has been stirred into a casserole dish then place your chicken on top.
- Add some pepper and salt to the chicken and cook everything for 50 mins in the oven.
- Enjoy.

Amount per serving (6 total)

Timing Information:

Preparation	10 m
Cooking	50 m
Total Time	1 h

Nutritional Information:

Calories	394 kcal
Fat	22.3 g
Carbohydrates	28g
Protein	18.9 g
Cholesterol	100 mg
Sodium	513 mg

* Percent Daily Values are based on a 2,000 calorie diet.

Easy Sweet Bake Chicken

Ingredients

- 1 (3 lb) whole chicken, cut into pieces
- 1/2 C. ketchup
- 1/4 C. water
- 1/4 C. packed brown sugar
- 1 (1 oz.) package dry onion soup mix

Directions

- Set your oven to 350 degrees before doing anything else.
- Get a bowl, mix: soup mix, ketchup, sugar, and water.
- Layer the chicken in a casserole dish.
- Top with the soup mix.
- Cook the mix in the oven for 65 mins.
- Enjoy.

Amount per serving (6 total)

Timing Information:

Preparation	10 m
Cooking	1 h
Total Time	1 h 10 m

Nutritional Information:

Calories	555 kcal
Fat	34.3 g
Carbohydrates	16.9g
Protein	42.9 g
Cholesterol	170 mg
Sodium	797 mg

* Percent Daily Values are based on a 2,000 calorie diet.

Italian Style Chicken

Ingredients

- 4 lbs dark meat chicken pieces
- 1 tbsp vegetable oil
- 5 cloves crushed garlic
- 1/2 C. all-purpose flour
- 1 tsp poultry seasoning
- 3 (4 oz.) links sweet Italian sausage, sliced
- 1 C. chopped onion
- 3 carrots, sliced
- 1/2 lb fresh mushrooms, sliced
- 1/2 tsp dried rosemary
- 1 C. red wine
- 1 (14.5 oz.) can whole peeled tomatoes
- salt and pepper to taste

Directions

- Get a bowl, combine: poultry seasoning and flour. Then coat the chicken with this mix.
- Stir fry half of your garlic in oil for 2 mins.
- Then brown the chicken in the oil for 5 mins before adding in the sausage and cooking for 2 more mins.
- Now add: the rest of garlic, onions, tomatoes, rosemary, carrots, wine, and mushrooms.

- Get everything boiling, once it is boiling, place a lid on the pan, set the heat to low, and cook the contents for 30 mins.
- Add in some pepper and salt and cook for 12 more mins.
- Let the chicken sit for 13 mins before serving.
- Enjoy.

Amount per serving (8 total)

Timing Information:

Preparation	10 m
Cooking	50 m
Total Time	1 h

Nutritional Information:

Calories	616 kcal
Fat	36.9 g
Carbohydrates	20.4g
Protein	43.5 g
Cholesterol	150 mg
Sodium	519 mg

* Percent Daily Values are based on a 2,000 calorie diet.

INDIAN STYLE CHICKEN IV

Ingredients

- 1 large onion, chopped
- 4 cloves garlic, chopped
- 1 slice fresh ginger root
- 1 tbsp olive oil
- 2 tsps ground cumin
- 1 tsp ground turmeric
- 1 tsp salt
- 1 tsp ground black pepper
- 1/2 tsp ground cardamom
- 1 (1 inch) piece cinnamon stick
- 1/4 tsp ground cloves
- 2 bay leaves
- 1/4 tsp ground nutmeg
- 6 skinless chicken thighs
- 1 (14.5 oz.) can whole peeled tomatoes, crushed

Directions

- In a blender puree: ginger, garlic, and onions.
- Then stir fry this mix in oil for 12 mins.
- Add in: nutmeg, cumin, bay leaves, turmeric, cloves, salt, cinnamon, pepper, and cardamom.
- Cook for 2 more mins before adding the chicken.
- Coat the chicken pieces with the spices and cook for 5 mins before adding the tomatoes and their juice.

- Get everything boiling, set the heat to low, and cook for 90 mins.
- Cook this with a lid on the pot.
- Enjoy.

Amount per serving (6 total)

Timing Information:

Preparation	15 m
Cooking	2 h
Total Time	2 h 15 m

Nutritional Information:

Calories	134 kcal
Fat	5.4 g
Carbohydrates	6.9g
Protein	14.7 g
Cholesterol	57 mg
Sodium	547 mg

* Percent Daily Values are based on a 2,000 calorie diet.

LEMONS AND OREGANO CHICKEN

Ingredients

- 7 chicken thighs
- 2 tsps dried oregano
- salt and pepper to taste
- 1/4 C. olive oil
- 1/2 lemon, juiced

Directions

- Set your oven to 450 degrees before doing anything else.
- Clean your chicken then top with pepper, salt, and oregano then layer the pieces into a casserole dish coated with nonstick spray.
- Get a bowl, combine: lemon juice and oil.
- Coat the chicken with half of the mix.
- Cook everything in the oven for 20 mins.
- Now flip the pieces and top the contents with the rest of the lemon mix.
- Cook the dish for 20 more mins in the oven.
- Enjoy.

Amount per serving (7 total)

Timing Information:

Preparation	10 m
Cooking	50 m
Total Time	1 h 10 m

Nutritional Information:

Calories	269 kcal
Fat	22.1 g
Carbohydrates	1.1g
Protein	16.4 g
Cholesterol	79 mg
Sodium	72 mg

* Percent Daily Values are based on a 2,000 calorie diet.

BUTTERY GARLIC AND PROSCIUTTO CHICKEN

Ingredients

- 2 tbsps butter or margarine, melted
- 6 chicken thighs
- salt and pepper to taste
- 6 slices prosciutto (thin sliced)
- 2 tbsps minced garlic, divided
- 1 C. sliced fresh mushrooms
- 1/4 C. dry white wine (optional)
- 1 C. sour cream

Directions

- Set your oven to 350 degrees before doing anything else.
- Top your chicken pieces with: 1 tbsp of garlic, pepper, and salt.
- Cover them with a wrapping of prosciutto.
- Coat your baking dish with some melted butter and then layer your chicken pieces in it.
- Now top everything with the rest of the garlic and the mushrooms.
- Cook the chicken and mushrooms in the oven for 65 mins.

- Add the liquid from the baking dish into a pot and add in sour cream and wine in it.
- Cook everything simmering for about 6 mins.
- Garnish your chicken liberally with the sauce when serving.
- Enjoy.

Amount per serving (6 total)

Timing Information:

Preparation	10 m
Cooking	1 h
Total Time	1 h 10 m

Nutritional Information:

Calories	383 kcal
Fat	30.8 g
Carbohydrates	3.3g
Protein	20.7 g
Cholesterol	119 mg
Sodium	399 mg

* Percent Daily Values are based on a 2,000 calorie diet.

Louisiana Style Chicken (Gumbo)

Ingredients

- 2 tbsps butter
- 2 cloves garlic
- 2 C. chopped onion
- 1/2 C. chopped green bell pepper
- 1/2 C. chopped celery
- 1 lb okra, chopped
- 1/4 C. canola oil
- 1/4 C. all-purpose flour
- 1 lb chicken thighs
- 1 lb andouille sausage links
- 2 C. water
- 6 C. chicken broth
- 2 lbs fresh shrimp, peeled and deveined
- 1 sprig fresh thyme
- 3 tsps chopped fresh parsley
- 1/2 tsp salt
- 1/4 tsp cayenne pepper
- 1/2 tsp hot pepper sauce (e.g. Tabasco(TM))
- 1/2 tsp file powder (optional)

Directions

- Stir fry your: okra, garlic, celery, onions, and bell peppers in butter until brown.
- Then place it all into a bowl.
- Add in your sausage and brown them.
- Place the sausages to the side as well.

- Now add in veggie oil to the pan and fry the chicken for 22 mins, flipping them every so often.
- Once the chicken is done, place it in the bowl too.
- Add some flour to the pan and begin to stir the mix over a low level of heat and continue cooking and stirring for about 30 mins until it becomes brown now add in water (two C.) as well as: pepper, garlic, and onions.
- Increase the heat and get everything boiling.
- Once everything is boiling add the broth and get it boiling again, now reduce the heat to low and let the mix simmer.
- Chunk your chicken and pour the pieces into the simmering broth. Now add the sausage and okra mix.
- Let this gently cook for 60 mins.
- Simultaneously boil your rice in 2 C. of water to a boil, then place a lid on the pot, and set the heat to a low level.
- Let the rice cook for 22 mins then add in the shrimp and: hot sauce, thyme, cayenne, parsley, and salt.
- Cook for 22 more mins before shutting the heat and adding in the file powder.
- Serve the rice with a topping of chicken, sausage and okra.
- Enjoy.

Amount per serving (10 total)

Timing Information:

Preparation	45 m
Cooking	3 h
Total Time	3 h 45 m

Nutritional Information:

Calories	435 kcal
Fat	27.7 g
Carbohydrates	11.3g
Protein	33.8 g
Cholesterol	202 mg
Sodium	1295 mg

* Percent Daily Values are based on a 2,000 calorie diet.

THAI STYLE CHICKEN

Ingredients

- 3 lemongrass stalks, bottom two-thirds of tender inner bulbs only, thinly sliced
- 4 cloves garlic, chopped
- 1 (4 inch) piece fresh ginger root, chopped
- 4 C. chicken broth
- 1 tbsp vegetable oil
- 2 1/2 lbs skinless, boneless chicken thighs, cut into chunks
- 12 oz. fresh white mushrooms, quartered
- 2 tsps red curry paste
- 3 tbsps fish sauce
- 1 lime, juiced
- 2 (14 oz.) cans coconut milk
- 1 red onion, sliced
- 1/2 bunch cilantro, roughly chopped
- 1 lime, cut into wedges, for serving
- 1 fresh jalapeno pepper, sliced into rings

Directions

- Get the following boiling: broth, lemon grass, ginger, and garlic.
- Set the heat to a low level and cook for 35 mins.
- Drain out the broth and place everything to the side, throw away the other contents.

- Get a big pot and stir fry your chicken for 7 mins in veggie oil then add the mushrooms and fry for 7 more mins.
- Now add: lime juice, curry paste, and fish sauce.
- Add the broth as well as the coconut milk.
- Get everything boiling, then lower the heat, and gently cook for 22 mins.
- Remove any excess oils then add in the onions and cook for 7 more mins.
- Shut the heat and top the contents with some cilantro.
- Serve the soup with some jalapenos, more cilantro, and lime pieces.
- Enjoy.

Amount per serving (6 total)

Timing Information:

Preparation	15 m
Cooking	1 h
Total Time	1 h 15 m

Nutritional Information:

Calories	596 kcal
Fat	44.8 g
Carbohydrates	14.3g
Protein	41 g
Cholesterol	114 mg
Sodium	1207 mg

* Percent Daily Values are based on a 2,000 calorie diet.

CREAM OF EVERYTHING CHICKEN

Ingredients

- 1 tbsp butter
- 8 skinless chicken thighs
- salt and pepper to taste
- 1 (10.75 oz.) can condensed cream of celery soup
- 1 (10.75 oz.) can condensed cream of mushroom soup
- 1 (5 oz.) jar pimento-stuffed green olives
- 1 (8 oz.) package sliced fresh mushrooms
- 1 1/4 C. Chablis wine
- 1 tbsp all-purpose flour

Directions

- Top your chicken with some pepper and salt then brown it all over in butter for 5 mins. Then add it into a crock pot.
- Cook your celery soup and mushroom soup in the same pan and heat it up for 3 mins.
- Then top the chicken with it.
- Add in the flour, olives, wine, and mushrooms to the slow cooker as well and stir everything evenly.

- Place a lid on the slow cooker and with low heat cook everything for 9 hrs.
- Enjoy.

Amount per serving (4 total)

Timing Information:

Preparation	25 m
Cooking	8 h
Total Time	8 h 25 m

Nutritional Information:

Calories	528 kcal
Fat	23.8 g
Carbohydrates	15.1g
Protein	49.9 g
Cholesterol	1207 mg
Sodium	2308 mg

* Percent Daily Values are based on a 2,000 calorie diet.

Moroccan Style Chicken (Tagine) (Slow Cooker)

Ingredients

- 2 tbsps olive oil
- 8 skinless, boneless chicken thighs, cut into 1-inch pieces
- 1 eggplant, cut into 1 inch cubes
- 2 large onions, thinly sliced
- 4 large carrots, thinly sliced
- 1/2 C. dried cranberries
- 1/2 C. chopped dried apricots
- 2 C. chicken broth
- 2 tbsps tomato paste
- 2 tbsps lemon juice
- 2 tbsps all-purpose flour
- 2 tsps garlic salt
- 1 1/2 tsps ground cumin
- 1 1/2 tsps ground ginger
- 1 tsp cinnamon
- 3/4 tsp ground black pepper
- 1 C. water
- 1 C. couscous

Directions

- Brown your chicken in olive oil along with the eggplants as well.
- Once everything is browned place the mix in the crock pot.

- Add the following to the chicken: apricots, onions, cranberries, and carrots.
- Get a bowl, combine: black pepper, broth, cinnamon, tomato paste, ginger, lemon juice, cumin, flour, and garlic salt.
- Add the wet mix to the slow cooker as well.
- Place a lid on the crock pot and cook the mix for 5 hrs on high.
- When 1 hour is left in the cooking time get your water boiling. Once it is boiling add in the couscous.
- Place a lid on the pot, and shut the heat.
- Let the couscous stand in the water for 7 mins. Then stir it.
- Serve the chicken on top of the couscous.
- Enjoy.

Amount per serving (8 total)

Timing Information:

Preparation	30 m
Cooking	5 h
Total Time	5 h 30 m

Nutritional Information:

Calories	380 kcal
Fat	15.2 g
Carbohydrates	38.5g
Protein	22.3 g
Cholesterol	65 mg
Sodium	571 mg

* Percent Daily Values are based on a 2,000 calorie diet.

ITALIAN STYLE CHICKEN II

Ingredients

- 15 chicken thighs
- 8 large potatoes, peeled and quartered
- 1 C. vegetable oil, or as needed
- 1/2 C. wine vinegar
- 5 lemons, juiced
- 10 cloves crushed garlic
- 2 tbsps dried oregano
- 2 tbsps dried parsley
- 1 onion, minced
- salt and pepper to taste

Directions

- Set your oven to 350 degrees before doing anything else.
- Fry your potatoes in oil until golden.
- Get a bowl, combine: half a C. of frying oil, vinegar, pepper, lemon juice, salt, garlic, onion, parsley, and oregano.
- Now layer your chicken in a casserole dish.

- Surround the chicken with the potatoes and then top the chicken with the wet mix.
- Cook everything in the oven for 80 mins.
- Baste the chicken at least 3 times throughout the cooking time.
- Enjoy.

Amount per serving (15 total)

Timing Information:

Preparation	15 m
Cooking	1 h 15 m
Total Time	1 h 30 m

Nutritional Information:

Calories	275 kcal
Fat	8.4 g
Carbohydrates	33.3g
Protein	19.1 g
Cholesterol	58 mg
Sodium	64 mg

* Percent Daily Values are based on a 2,000 calorie diet.

THAI STYLE CHICKEN II

Ingredients

- 1 C. soy sauce
- 8 cloves garlic, minced
- 1 tbsp minced fresh ginger root
- 2 tbsps hot pepper sauce
- 2 lbs skinless chicken thighs
- 1 tbsp sesame oil
- 1 tbsp brown sugar
- 1 onion, sliced
- 1/2 C. water
- 4 tbsps crunchy peanut butter
- 2 tbsps green onions, chopped

Directions

- Get a bowl, combine: hot sauce, soy sauce, chicken, ginger, and garlic.
- Cover the chicken pieces evenly with the mix and then place a covering over the bowl.
- Place everything in the fridge for 2 hours.

- Heat your sesame oil with some brown sugar in it until smooth then stir fry your onions in it for 7 mins.
- Combine in: the chicken and cook for 7 more mins flipping the chicken after 3 mins of frying.
- Add the marinade, and some water and get everything boiling.
- Once everything is boiling set the heat to low and let the contents cook for 22 mins. Now combine in the peanut butter and cook for 12 more mins.
- When serving your chicken top it liberally with sauce and also some chives.
- Enjoy.

Amount per serving (4 total)

Timing Information:

Preparation	20 m
Cooking	30 m
Total Time	50 m

Nutritional Information:

Calories	466 kcal
Fat	20.5 g
Carbohydrates	16.8g
Protein	53.4 g
Cholesterol	1188 mg
Sodium	3930 mg

* Percent Daily Values are based on a 2,000 calorie diet.

CREOLE STYLE CHICKEN I

Ingredients

- 8 chicken thighs
- 1/4 lb cooked ham, cut into one inch cubes
- 1 (16 oz.) can diced tomatoes
- 1 green bell pepper, chopped
- 6 green onions, chopped
- 1 (6 oz.) can tomato paste
- 1 tsp salt
- 2 dashes hot pepper sauce
- 2 C. water
- 1 C. uncooked long grain white rice
- 1/2 lb Polish sausage, sliced diagonally

Directions

- Put the following in your crock pot: hot sauce, chicken, salt, ham, tomato paste, tomatoes, onions, and bell peppers.
- Place a lid on the slow cooker and with low heat let the contents cook for 5 hrs.

- Get your rice and water boiling then place a lid on the pot, set the heat to low, and let it cook for 22 mins.
- Add the sausage and the rice to the crock pot and continue cooking for 40 mins with a high level of heat. At this point the sausage should be completely done.
- Enjoy.

Amount per serving (8 total)

Timing Information:

Preparation	15 m
Cooking	5 h 20 m
Total Time	5 h 35 m

Nutritional Information:

Calories	389 kcal
Fat	19.2 g
Carbohydrates	27.9g
Protein	24.5 g
Cholesterol	81 mg
Sodium	1083 mg

* Percent Daily Values are based on a 2,000 calorie diet.

Thai Style Chicken III

Ingredients

- 3/4 C. hot salsa
- 1/4 C. chunky peanut butter
- 3/4 C. light coconut milk
- 2 tbsps lime juice
- 1 tbsp soy sauce
- 1 tsp white sugar
- 2 tbsps grated fresh ginger
- 2 lbs skinless chicken thighs
- 1/2 C. chopped peanuts, for topping
- 2 tbsps chopped cilantro, for topping

Directions

- Add the following to your slow cooker: ginger, salsa, sugar, peanut butter, soy sauce, coconut milk, and lime juice.
- Add in the chicken as well and cook everything for 9 hours with a low level of heat.
- When serving the chicken add a topping of cilantro and peanuts.
- Enjoy.

Amount per serving (4 total)

Timing Information:

Preparation	15 m
Cooking	8 h
Total Time	8 h 15 m

Nutritional Information:

Calories	562 kcal
Fat	35.9 g
Carbohydrates	13.7g
Protein	47.6 g
Cholesterol	137 mg
Sodium	860 mg

* Percent Daily Values are based on a 2,000 calorie diet.

CHILI PEPPERS AND MONTEREY CHICKEN (MEXICAN STYLE)

Ingredients

- 15 boneless, skinless chicken thighs
- 1 (26 oz.) can condensed cream of chicken soup
- 2 cloves garlic, chopped (optional)
- 1 (16 oz.) container sour cream
- 1 (7 oz.) can diced green chili peppers
- 15 flour tortillas
- 3 1/2 C. shredded Monterey Jack cheese
- 1 (10 oz.) can sliced black olives (optional)
- chives for garnish (optional)
- black pepper to taste

Directions

- Boil your chicken in water for 12 mins. Then remove all the liquid and chunk the chicken when it is cool enough.
- Place everything into a bowl.
- Add to the chicken: chilies, soup, sour cream, and garlic.

- Coat your crock pot with nonstick spray then layer pieces of ripped tortillas at the bottom. Now layer half of the chicken mix, half of cheese, and then the soup over the tortillas.
- Continue layering until all of ingredients have been used up.
- Now add a final layering of olives.
- Cook the contents with a low level of heat for 5 hours.
- Enjoy.

Amount per serving (10 total)

Timing Information:

Preparation	30 m
Cooking	4 h
Total Time	4 h 30 m

Nutritional Information:

Calories	824 kcal
Fat	44 g
Carbohydrates	66.4g
Protein	40 g
Cholesterol	123 mg
Sodium	1931 mg

* Percent Daily Values are based on a 2,000 calorie diet.

Vinegar and Salt Chicken
(English Style)

Ingredients

- 2 C. cider vinegar
- 1 C. vegetable oil
- 1 egg, lightly beaten
- 3 tsps salt
- 1 tsp poultry seasoning
- 8 boneless chicken thighs, with skin

Directions

- Get a bowl, combine: poultry seasoning, chicken, vinegar, salt, veggie oil, and beaten eggs.
- Stir everything to coat the chicken and then place a covering of plastic on the bowl and let it sit in the fridge for 2 hrs.
- Set your oven to 350 degrees before doing anything else.
- Layer your chicken pieces in a casserole dish and top them with half of the marinade.

- Cook everything in the oven for 35 mins then remove any liquids.
- Now cook for 17 more mins until the chicken is fully done and a bit crispy.
- Enjoy.

Amount per serving (8 total)

Timing Information:

Preparation	15 m
Cooking	45 m
Total Time	2 h

Nutritional Information:

Calories	418 kcal
Fat	37.6 g
Carbohydrates	0.7g
Protein	16.6 g
Cholesterol	82 mg
Sodium	937 mg

* Percent Daily Values are based on a 2,000 calorie diet.

ARABIC STYLE CHICKEN

Ingredients

- 1 tsp olive oil
- 1 C. sliced onion
- 2 1/2 lbs skinless, boneless chicken thighs
- 1 tbsp garam masala
- 1/2 tsp curry powder
- 1/2 C. red wine
- 2 tbsps red wine vinegar
- 1 C. fat-free, reduced-sodium chicken broth

Directions

- Stir fry your onions in olive oil for 9 mins then place them to the side.
- Turn up the heat and top your chicken with some curry and masala before laying it in the pan and browning it for 5 mins.
- Now flip the chicken and cook it for 5 more mins.
- Add in the wine and vinegar and cook for 2 mins before scraping the bottom of the pan.
- Add the broth and onions and get everything boiling.
- Once it is boiling place a lid on the pot, set the heat to low, and let the contents gently simmer for 22 mins.
- Enjoy.

Amount per serving (6 total)

Timing Information:

Preparation	10 m
Cooking	35 m
Total Time	45 m

Nutritional Information:

Calories	331 kcal
Fat	19.7 g
Carbohydrates	3.6g
Protein	29.8 g
Cholesterol	106 mg
Sodium	95 mg

* Percent Daily Values are based on a 2,000 calorie diet.

AFRICAN STYLE CHICKEN

Ingredients

- 12 chicken thighs
- 1 (12 oz.) jar hot chutney
- 1 (1 oz.) package dry onion soup mix

Directions

- Set your oven to 375 degrees before doing anything else.
- Get a bowl, combine: soup and chutney.
- Top your chicken with some pepper and salt and lay them into a casserole dish.
- Top the chicken pieces with your wet mix and cook them in the oven for 65 mins.
- Baste the chicken at least once with any drippings
- Enjoy.

Amount per serving (6 total)

Timing Information:

Preparation	10 m
Cooking	1 h 10 m
Total Time	1 h 20 m

Nutritional Information:

Calories	495 kcal
Fat	29 g
Carbohydrates	25g
Protein	33.5 g
Cholesterol	158 mg
Sodium	566 mg

* Percent Daily Values are based on a 2,000 calorie diet.

Parsley, Peppers, and Sweet Onions Chicken

Ingredients

- 3 tbsps vegetable oil
- 2 red bell peppers, seeded and diced
- 2 large sweet onions, peeled and cut into wedges
- 1 1/2 lbs skinless, boneless chicken boneless thighs - cut into cubes
- 2 cloves garlic, minced
- 1 pinch ground cayenne pepper
- 1 lemon, juiced
- 2 tbsps butter
- 2 tbsps chopped fresh parsley
- salt and pepper to taste

Directions

- Stir fry your onions and bell peppers in oil until tender then place them to the side.
- Combine the chicken into the pan and brown them before adding the red pepper and garlic.
- Cook for 3 mins with a low heat then add in lemon juice and scrape the bottom of the pan.
- Combine in your butter and let it melt.

- Now add the pepper mix back into the pan as well.
- Cook for about 4 more mins before topping with parsley and some pepper and salt.
- Enjoy.

Amount per serving (4 total)

Timing Information:

Preparation	10 m
Cooking	40 m
Total Time	1 h 10 m

Nutritional Information:

Calories	420 kcal
Fat	18.6 g
Carbohydrates	22.1g
Protein	42.2 g
Cholesterol	114 mg
Sodium	163 mg

* Percent Daily Values are based on a 2,000 calorie diet.

Japanese Style Chicken III

Ingredients

- 2 C. uncooked jasmine rice
- 4 C. water
- 4 skinless, boneless chicken thighs, cut into small pieces
- 1 onion, cut in half and sliced
- 2 C. dashi stock, made with dashi powder
- 1/4 C. soy sauce
- 3 tbsps mirin (Japanese rice wine)
- 3 tbsps brown sugar
- 4 eggs

Directions

- Run your rice under water then add them to 4 C. of fresh water in a pot and get it boiling.
- Once everything is boiling place a lid on the pot, set the heat to low, and let the contents simmer for 22 mins.
- Get a pan and coat it with nonstick spray.
- Cook your chicken until fully done, in the pan, while covered, for 7 mins, then add the onions and cook for 7 more mins.

- Add in the following: sugar, stock, mirin, and soy sauce.
- Get the mixture boiling while stirring and then let it thicken for about 9 to 12 mins.
- Beat your eggs and then add them to the stock.
- Place a lid on the pan and set the heat to low. Let the eggs poach for 7 mins or until cooked.
- Now shut the heat.
- Get a bowl for serving and add some rice, 1/4 of the chicken mix, and half a C. of soup.
- Enjoy.

Amount per serving (4 total)

Timing Information:

Preparation	15 m
Cooking	25 m
Total Time	40 m

Nutritional Information:

Calories	688 kcal
Fat	14.6 g
Carbohydrates	97.9g
Protein	35.3 g
Cholesterol	208 mg
Sodium	1226 mg

* Percent Daily Values are based on a 2,000 calorie diet.

CRANBERRIES AND ONIONS CHICKEN

Ingredients

- 6 chicken thighs
- 1 (16 oz.) can cranberry sauce
- 1 (8 oz.) bottle Russian-style salad dressing
- 1 packet dry onion soup mix

Directions

- Set your oven to 350 degrees before doing anything else.
- Get a bowl, combine: soup mix, dressing, and cranberry sauce.
- Coat a casserole dish with nonstick spray and layer your chicken pieces in it. Cover the chicken with the wet mix.
- Place some foil around the casserole dish and cook it in the oven for 90 mins.
- When 20 mins is left take off the foil and finish the baking.
- Enjoy.

Amount per serving (7 total)

Timing Information:

Preparation	15 m
Cooking	1 h 45 m
Total Time	2 h

Nutritional Information:

Calories	397 kcal
Fat	20.8 g
Carbohydrates	38.4g
Protein	15 g
Cholesterol	68 mg
Sodium	828 mg

* Percent Daily Values are based on a 2,000 calorie diet.

Thanks for Reading! Join the Club and Keep on Cooking with 6 More Cookbooks....

http://bit.ly/1TdrStv

 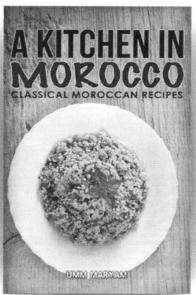 

To grab the box sets simply follow the link mentioned above, or tap one of book covers.

This will take you to a page where you can simply enter your email address and a PDF version of the box sets will be emailed to you.

Hope you are ready for some serious cooking!

http://bit.ly/1TdrStv

COME ON...
LET'S BE FRIENDS :)

We adore our readers and love connecting with them socially.

Like BookSumo on Facebook and let's get social!

Facebook

And also check out the BookSumo Cooking Blog.

Food Lover Blog

Made in the USA
Middletown, DE
18 May 2018